PRESENTED TO

_____

FROM

_____

DATE PRESENTED

_____

"Do it as you can, until you can do it as you would."
– John Wesley

SEVEN THINGS

JOHN WESLEY

Expected Us to Do
FOR KIDS

Seven Things John Wesley Expected Us to Do for Kids

Copyright © 2016 by Cokesbury.
All rights reserved.

Editor: Daphna Flegal
Designer: Jim Carlton

Art—p. 4: Shutterstock®; all other art: Mark Whitaker/MTWDesign.net

ISBN: 9781501821288
PACP10041838-02

16 17 18 19 20 21 22 23 24 25—10 9 8 7 6 5 4 3 2 1
Printed in the United States of America

SEVEN THINGS

JOHN WESLEY

Expected Us to Do
FOR KIDS

Christopher Miles Ritter

Cokesbury

Nashville

I dedicate this book to Becky,
my partner in life and ministry,
whose huge heart for children
is a constant source of inspiration.

CONTENTS

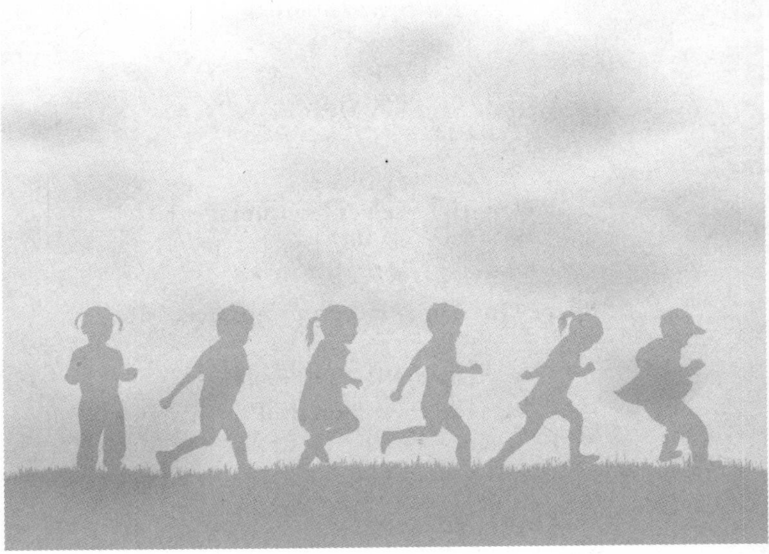

INTRODUCTION

*"Gift or no gift, you are to do this, or else you are
not called to be a Methodist Preacher." —John Wesley*

JOHN WESLEY'S INDEX FINGER perched uncomfortably on the
end of my nose.

Before we get to that, let me first say that I am glad you are here. The fact
that you picked up this book about what we should be doing for kids
tells me that you already feel children are important. I bet you believe
the church should be investing in young lives. You might even be open to
personally helping make that happen. I share your convictions. In fact, one
of the historic questions I was asked as I joined the ranks of the clergy was,

> *"Will you diligently instruct the children in every place?"*
> *I said I would ... and I meant it.*

Long before I was ever ordained, I worked to make sure kids were
ministered to in and through the congregations I served. My very first
ministry position was when I was the tender age of eighteen. Fresh out
of high school, I was supplied to three patient congregations in extreme
Southern Illinois as their pastor. One of my churches, Center United
Methodist Church, had six people (when everyone was there), no
children, and the outhouses behind the church had caved in. Luther's
Chapel UMC had twelve seasoned citizens in attendance, functional
outhouses, but no children. Cypress UMC had two dozen attendees,

indoor plumbing, and a couple of kids. After long consideration, I decided to start my children's ministry efforts in Cypress. An outreach during the kids' Easter break attracted over twenty children to the church. Several prayed to accept Christ. Becky, my high-school-sweetheart-turned-bride, started a children's church program that continued the momentum. We were off and running.

As the ministry years continued, my wife and I loaded the van for church camp, knocked on doors inviting kids to church, and put on Christmas pageants. Becky once hosted a girls' sleepover at the parsonage and thirty-five squealing girls showed up with their sleeping bags. (I evacuated to my mom's house that night.)

We eventually jumped from serving small to medium-sized congregations and tried to continue the emphasis on children's ministry. We started a mid-week program in my first appointment after seminary and eventually reached a hundred kids each week, a quarter of the local elementary school. I even took a bucket of slime over my head during vacation Bible school when the kids reached their giving goal for the week's mission project.

As I came to serve larger congregations, my personal role shifted to making sure the church was family-friendly. I recruited great Sunday school teachers and called children to the altar during worship for children's messages. Becky became a children's ministry director of infinitely higher quality than I would ever hope to be. The net result over the years was that ministry to children morphed from something I did to something I encouraged. The transition felt quite natural. I sort of "graduated" from the children's department. No books on church leadership told me I should do otherwise. Delegation is a pastoral virtue. My time was better spent preaching, leading staff, raising money, and reaching adults.

I still thought I was doing a fairly decent job of living up, by extension, to the promise I made at ordination. Recently, however, I ran across a definition of what "diligently instruct the children" meant to the guy who wrote the question. My perspective was forever changed.

THE MAN AND THE REVIVAL

As a United Methodist, I stand in one of the distributaries flowing from an river of spiritual revival that started in eighteenth-century England. The man at the fountainhead of this outpouring was an Anglican priest turned evangelist named John Wesley. The reason you have heard of him is because he had the wisdom to recognize a unique work of the Holy Spirit and build an entrepreneurial organization equipped to keep it going. A big part of his efforts involved summoning a fiery host of both ordained and lay preachers to join his work of taking Jesus to people who were not being reached by traditional means.

As something of a history geek, I recently found myself reading the record of the early conversations Wesley had with the preachers "in connexion" with him. These Large Minutes were written in question-and-answer format (Wesley providing the answers) and offer an important glimpse into the development of the movement. The topics were both doctrinal and practical: "What to teach, how to teach, and what to do." Starting in 1768, one of the questions asked was this: "But what can we do for the rising generation?" In other words, "What about the kids?"

Wesley's response was pregnant with urgency:

> *Unless we take care of this, the present Revival will be* res unius aetatis *[a thing of only one age].... Who will labor herein? Let him who is zealous for God and the souls of men begin now.*

Wesley saw that the Methodist revival would be a single-generation phenomenon without intentional focus given to children and youth. His words do more than just reveal his strategic mind as chief engineer of the movement. He transformed a what question by answering it with a who and a when:

> *Let him who is zealous for God and the souls of men begin now.*

Here was an inescapable call to action. Wesley was telling his preachers, "The who is you and the when is now!"

GIFT OR NO GIFT

Children's ministry is perhaps the most specialized compartment of the church. You only need to wander through the building of any growing congregation and you can readily identify the area intended for kids. Most every church I have served has been blessed with a small but dedicated corps of exceptional servants who show up to serve the young. These are the faithful souls who show up to change diapers in the nursery, wrangle restless Sunday schoolers, and glue macaroni noodles to things for a vacation Bible school craft. To show our appreciation to them, we bring them in front of the church and clap for them at least once a year, whether they ask for it or not. After all, here are special people with special gifts operating in a special field.

In reading the Large Minutes, I was not surprised to learn that Wesley believed in ministry to children. I was shocked, however, to learn who he assigned to the task. He said I should do it. When I was asked at ordination, "Will you diligently instruct the children in every place?" I assumed it meant that I would, generally speaking, oversee the educational enterprise of the congregation. Wesley, however, meant for preachers to teach children personally, regularly, systematically, and intentionally. What if we decline, defer, delegate, or otherwise dodge?

> *"If you do not do this, you are not called*
> *to be a Methodist Preacher."*

Ouch. John Wesley's finger made contact with the tip of my nose.

Did my hero, John Wesley, just tell me, the great delegator, that I didn't have the right to call myself a Methodist preacher if I didn't spend time with children? Didn't he realize that my time could be better spent recruiting qualified—yes, better qualified—people to do it for me? He refused to let me off the hook. The instruction continued:

> *Gift or no gift, you are to do this, or else you are not called to be*
> *a Methodist Preacher. Do it as you can till you can do it as you*
> *would. Pray earnestly for the gift and use the means for it.*

It was almost as if Wesley peered through time and predicted "That's not my gift" would become the biggest cop-out in the Body of Christ. We love to use Paul's teaching on spiritual gifts to shift responsibility onto unnamed people with "more suitable gifts." Used correctly, this excuse can get you out of evangelism, tithing, and singing audibly during worship . . . all while sounding quite spiritual. We neglect, however, the fact that the apostle taught the greatest gifts are those that build others up. We each are to "eagerly desire," seek, and pray for these gifts (1 Cor. 12:31) as living sacrifices for our Lord (Romans 12).

Wesley revealed "That's not my gift" for what it often is . . . a nice Christian way of saying, "Go find someone else." He said that if I am no good at ministering to children, I am to keep getting better by practice and I am to pray for greater gifts in this area. The one thing we preachers must not do, according to Wesley, is stop ministering directly to children or completely delegate the task to others.

I want to pause here and speak to any folks who might be crimping this page to show their pastor. The reason why the Large Minutes told preachers they need to minister to children is because the Minutes are written to preachers. This should in no way be construed to say that preachers should be the only ones, or even the primary ones, teaching children. But for Wesley, the question of who was not nearly as important as the question of when. "Let him who is zealous for God and the soul of men begin now." The who is me because the when is now.

I often think about my Grandma Virginia, who worked assembling aircraft in the early 1940's. Her training and gifts were in home economics, not riveting. Why did she involve herself in such an ill-suited task? A war was on. The need was urgent. The workers were few. She jumped in, did what she could, and got better as she went along. I think this is the spirit in which Wesley called his preachers to instruct the young. The task is too large and urgent to restrict it to the equipped, the gifted, or even the willing.

Of course, there are people who are disqualified from working with children directly. I know folks whose history is such that they could not pass the various screenings we use for children's workers in our church, nor would they attempt to do so. They voluntarily stay away from kids, yet find other ways to be supportive of the educational enterprise of the congregation. Some work diligently in adult ministries to free up others to work with children. The vast majority of us, however, could do more for the rising generation if we jettisoned our excellent excuses.

SEVEN EXPECTATIONS

Wesley gave his conferencing Methodists the minimum expectation for their work as it related to children:

> *WHERE there are ten children in a Society, we must meet them at least an hour every week; talk with them whenever we see any of them at home; pray in earnest for them; diligently instruct and vehemently exhort all parents at their own houses. Some will say, "I have no gift for this." Gift or no gift, you are to do this, or else you are not called to be a Methodist Preacher. Do it as you can, till you can do it as you would. Pray earnestly for the gift, and use every help God hath put into your way, in order to attain it. Preach expressly on the education of children when you make the Collection for Kingswood School.*

I find here seven instructions Wesley gave to the preachers (and, by extension, the whole Methodist/Wesleyan movement) that will form the outline for the rest of this book. Along the way, we are going to meet in each chapter a child God might be calling you to personally reach. I hope you, like me, start to feel John Wesley's finger on the end of your nose. Better still, I pray that the Holy Spirit stirs your heart to love the rising generation toward Jesus, one child at a time.

"Let him who is zealous for God and the souls of men begin now."

—John Wesley

ONE

Teach Them Intentionally

BEFORE MY MOM'S retirement, her career in education spanned three decades. I sat in her classes all four years of high school. We both survived. Right next door to mom's classroom was her sister, who taught typing and bookkeeping. My own sister, Cindy, is a kindergarten teacher. After my dad's untimely passing, my mom married Robert, who is now retired from teaching and school administration. I have a great-uncle who was an agriculture professor and a great-grandma who taught in a one-room school. My cousins, Karen, Sandra, and Kathy, are all teachers. I am married to Becky, a teacher. My daughter, Hannah, and I also have undergraduate degrees in elementary education. Suffice it to say that teaching is sort of the family business.

Even from my family's perspective, it is difficult to imagine someone with a bigger investment in education than John Wesley. He perhaps spent more time on education throughout his ministry than any other single concern. Hundreds of volumes have been written on his work of building schools, advocating for educational reform, expanding access to education, and editing textbooks.

Full disclosure: No one ever confused John Wesley with Walt Disney. His vociferous commitment to hard work and diligence made him opposed to recess or any other form of child's play. Sometimes it seems like he viewed childhood, like the flu, as a condition one should hope to get over as soon as possible. This outlook, very much reflective of the era in which he lived, stands in stark contrast to our culture, where childhood is something to be exalted and, when possible, extended. In spite of his hard edge, it is undeniable that Wesley valued children and their souls.

One of my favorite scenes from Wesley's life is depicted in his journal from Tuesday, February 8, 1779, at Stockton-on-Tees in County Durham. After he preached on his favorite theme, "The kingdom of heaven is at hand," a revival broke out among a group of over sixty children, aged six to fourteen. Wesley recorded:

As soon as I came down from the [preaching] desk I was enclosed by a body of children, one of whom and another sunk down upon their knees until they were all kneeling, so I kneeled down myself and began praying for them. Abundance of people ran back into the house. The fire kindled and ran from heart to heart till few, if any, were unaffected. Is not this a new thing in the earth? God begins his work in children! Thus it has been also in Cornwall, Manchester, and Epworth. Thus the flame spreads to those of riper years till, at length, they all know him and praise him from the least unto the greatest.

The image of the seventy-five-year-old Wesley kneeling in the middle of a group of children reveals the tender, pastoral heart that is sometimes obscured by his more strident educational theories. He clearly valued the simple faith of children as a catalyst for the work of the Holy Spirit.

TEACH CHILDREN WELL

Long before Crosby, Stills, Nash, and Young were singing about it, Moses was telling Israel to "Teach [these words] to your children, talking about them when you are at home and when you are away, when you lie down and when you rise" (Deut. 11:19). Wise Solomon advised: "Train children in the right way, and when old, they will not stray" (Prov. 22:6).

The notion that children should be taught is apparent to those with even one eye to the future. Wesley was merely stating the obvious when he said that without ministry to children, the Methodist movement would be short-lived. The value placed on the training of the young, however, was not some utilitarian concern for institutional survival. The Wesleyan why for teaching children is spiritual and bears the weight and urgency of eternity. Kids matter to God. Kids need Jesus.

In his sermon "On Family Religion," Wesley reminded parents that children are

> *immortal spirits whom God hath, for a time, entrusted to your care, that you may train them up in all holiness, and fit them for the enjoyment of God in eternity. This is a glorious and important trust, seeing our soul is of more value than all the world beside. Every child, therefore, you are to watch over with the utmost care.*

The souls of children are eternal and precious. They are also at risk. Wesley was no Pollyanna about either human nature or human nurture apart from God's grace. The environment in which children are raised can never be spiritually neutral. A competition is constantly being waged for their souls. Consider the countless media messages confronting us about values, beauty, importance, and worth. Independent of Christ, our culture has developed answers to the questions of who and what matters. Our children are being indoctrinated into a system of values whether we teach them or not.

Children also face threats from within. Wesley saw the human spirit, apart from grace, as inherently bent toward destruction. You may have noticed that children don't need to be taught to be selfish. It comes quite naturally. They can, however, be taught to share. God's first lesson to humanity outside of Eden speaks to the danger and opportunity faced by every son of Adam and daughter of Eve: "Sin is lurking at the door; its desire is for you, but you must master it" (Gen. 4:7).

EDUCATION IS FORMATION

The Kingdom of God is an insurgency in a larger, fallen system of living. Education, for Wesley, was more about formation than information. His sermon "On the Education of Children" includes seven natural but deadly sins that Christian spiritual formation will help a child overcome: Atheism, Self-Worship, Pride, Love of the World, Anger, Deviation from the Truth, and Living Contrary to Justice. The goal of Christian education for Wesley was nothing less than Christian discipleship:

> *An education under Pythagorus or Socrates had no other end but to teach children to think and act as Pythagoras and Socrates did. And is it not reasonable to suppose that a Christian education should have no other end but to teach them to think, and judge, and act according [to Christ]?*

A focus on formation does not mean that the content of the faith was in some way neglected. Wesley prepared tools that anyone could use to teach children theological truths. His Lessons for Children was a series of two hundred Old Testament Bible stories for use with younger children. Every Methodist home was likewise encouraged to obtain a copy of Wesley's best-selling Instructions for Children, a thirty-nine-page catechism he adapted from a French source. These lessons for older children begin with the theological headers of God, creation, sin, redemption through the cross, and eternity. They then branch out into practical ways of living spiritually: how to regulate our desires, understanding, joy, and practice.

Information partnered with practical formation was Wesley's recipe for transformation. This works with adults, too.

TEACHABLE MOMENTS

Wesley instructed the preachers in connection with him to spend at least an hour each week meeting with the children of the Methodist society as a group. These gatherings were for formal, spiritual instruction personally delivered by the preacher to the children and supplemental to the instruction they were receiving at home. Being a disciplined spiritual movement and not a church, society meetings could only be attended by those who held a quarterly ticket, procured by demonstrating, under examination, their serious pursuit of God. The meetings for children, however, were ticketless. We might consider them a ministry of prevenient grace.

According to Barna Research, nearly half of all Americans who accept Jesus as their Savior do so before reaching the age of thirteen. The childhood years are the most fruitful for both evangelism and discipleship. Far from putting the pressure on pastors and church leaders, Barna notes that most young conversions happen through the influence of a family member or a friend, not at a church event. Some of the most important spiritual instruction happens outside the classroom.

It might be helpful to remember that organized children's ministry is a relatively new phenomenon in the history of the church. Although there have always been some teaching ministries led by the clergy, informal lay instruction, especially in families, has formed the core of the church's teaching enterprise throughout the centuries.

When it comes to teaching children, Wesley was convinced that the work is eternal, the needs are urgent, and the call is upon all of us regardless of how we might feel inadequate to the task. He expected all Methodists to teach children intentionally.

THE CHILD ON HER TIPTOES

I took my first trip to Liberia, West Africa, in 2012 with Mike Ashdown, a businessman from my church. I had been involved with the United Methodist Church in Liberia since 2004, soon after the end of the prolonged and brutal civil war there. During our visit we found the church there thriving spiritually amidst extreme poverty and a sluggish national recovery from the ravages of war.

Mike allowed me the freedom to roam wherever I wished, checking on projects and people I had only known through correspondence. It was wonderful. I asked our guide if she could show us the Christian frontier, a place where the message of Jesus was being brought to people who had never heard the Gospel. She led us across miles and miles of cratered roads, through a complicated international border crossing into what Liberian United Methodists call "The Guinea Ministry."

A neighbor to Liberia, Guinea received a sudden influx of refugees during the war years. The flood of desperate Liberians crossing the border created a humanitarian crisis. The United Methodist Committee on Relief responded and established a school and clinic to assist. The unexpected blessing of this crisis is that the Liberians, many of them United Methodists, organically planted fifteen new churches in Guinea, a nation where Christians represent a single-digit percentage of the population. The congregations survived even after their Liberian founders returned home. A new, indigenous, French-speaking church was taking root.

We toured the United Methodist School at Diecke, Guinea. As the principal walked with us through the cinder block campus, we saw the rooms where some six hundred students in khaki uniforms sat under the tutelage of their instructors. A large mural of Jesus dominated the wall of one of the classrooms. Back outside, I noticed a group of fifteen children standing on their tiptoes. They were not in uniforms like the rest, but were straining to peer into a classroom window. I questioned the principal and he told me that these were children whose families could not afford to send them to the school. They stood outside trying to catch a little of what the teacher was saying. Seeing children literally on the outside of opportunity hit me squarely in the gut. The kids noticed me and ran over to say bonjour to the large, pale-skinned visitor. I left them knowing I had experienced the call of the Holy Spirit to get those kids, somehow, on the other side of the classroom wall.

Back in Illinois, I shared the story of the "tiptoe children" with my church family, First United Methodist Church of Geneseo, and the H.O.P.E. Scholarship Program was born. H.O.P.E. is an acronym for Helping Others Pursue Education, and we currently send over seventy students to the Diecke United Methodist School on full scholarship. Over half of our HOPE scholars are girls whose access to education is somewhat stifled by the larger culture in Guinea. We are blessed to receive photos of our students and regular reports on their progress.

Wesley expected us to teach children intentionally. If you are not already in a teaching role with children, you may be wondering where to begin. Somewhere within your reach there is a child on her tiptoes, ready to learn. There is a saying that is sometimes attributed to Siddhartha Gautama, the Buddha: "When the student is ready, the teacher will appear." A Christian spin on this saying might be, "When a heart is hungry to learn, the Holy Spirit sends someone to teach." Maybe you are that someone for one child. We may only need to expand the definition of "our kids." There is a page at the back of this book to write down the name of a child God might be calling you to intentionally teach.

"Talk with them whenever we see any of them at home."

—John Wesley

TWO

Know Them Personally

GOD IS RELATIONAL. Relationship is the foundation of ministry. It was with this knowledge that Wesley mandated that each preacher's afternoons be spent visiting. In my denomination, vowing to "visit house to house" is still required for clergy membership in the conference. We preachers are sometimes fond of commenting that people nowadays, outside of a few shut-ins, don't really expect the pastor to show up at their door. In fact, most probably would prefer we don't!

It should be noted, however, that Wesley didn't tell preachers to visit because people might appreciate their company. Visitation was about evangelism and discipleship, not public relations. The home was and is the most important environment for spiritual growth and accountability. Preachers, as agents of the Kingdom, have vested interest in each home in their care being conducive to the work of the Holy Spirit.

As a format for home visits, Wesley recommended a system developed by English Puritan Richard Baxter. He made a uniquely Methodist contribution to the plan, however, by incorporating work with children. Preachers were not just to talk to the adults. They were also to have direct conversation with the children. Wesley's instructions paint a picture of the nature of the home visits:

> *After a few loving words spoken to all in the house, take each person [individually] into another room where you may deal closely with him about his sin and misery and duty. . . . Hear what the children have learned by heart. Choose some of the weightier points and see if they understand them. . . . With these you are to be exceedingly tender, lest they be discouraged. If you perceive they are troubled that they cannot answer, step in and take the burden off them, answering the question yourself. And do it thoroughly and plainly. Before you leave them, engage the head of each family to gather all his family together every Sunday before they go to bed and hear what they can repeat [from memory], and so continue until they have learned the Instructions perfectly. And afterwards, let him take care that they do not forget what they have learned. Do this in earnest and you will soon find what a work you take in hand undertaking to be a Travelling Preacher![1]*

John Wesley intended that there be meaningful, ongoing spiritual conversations happening between preachers and children. I think this expectation is particularly striking in light of the prevailing notion of his time that children should be seen and not heard. The spiritual condition of adults was an urgent matter. The spiritual needs and condition of the young were no less urgent. I also suspect there might be something about entering into the world of a child that has a formative effect on a preacher. Maybe a Christian leader is never more free than when he or she is investing time in someone who can offer no immediate benefit to the organization but is nevertheless essentially constituent of the Kingdom of God (Matt. 19:14).

KNOW THEM

If we hope to minister to children, we must first know them. Of course, there are the surface facts we all must wade through as we get to know anyone: What is your name? What is your family like? What do you like to do? What grade are you in?

But the ultimate goal is to get to the level of the heart. John Wesley always wanted to talk about the heart and to the heart. In speaking of ministry with children, he said,

> *We must get to the heart, or we do nothing.*[2]

Proverbs 4:23 says, "Keep your heart with all vigilance, for from it flow the springs of life." The realm of the spirit is the place from which we deliberate and decide. Unfortunately, many of us aren't very good at going there. While it is easier to remain on the surface, being a spiritual friend to children necessitates going deeper to the realm of hopes, fears, and faith. This requires trust. Trust takes time.

Andy Stanley is pastor of one of the largest congregations in the United States. In his book *When Work and Family Collide*, he shares five questions he used with his own young children to access a deeper level: Is everything OK in your heart? Did anyone hurt your feelings today? Are you mad at anyone? Did anyone break a promise to you? Is there anything I can do for you? Asking these sorts of questions when the time is right helps us to become a spiritual friend to children. The adults who made the biggest impact on my young life were the ones who were also willing to share their faith story and their heart with me.

PATIENCE

In teaching Methodist preachers the spirit in which they needed to do their work with children, John Wesley recalled the long-suffering instructions of his mother. He noted how his own father, frustrated in overhearing his wife's repetitive lessons, asked, "How could you have the patience to tell that blockhead the same thing twenty times over?" Her reply: "If I had told him only nineteen times, I would have wasted all my labor."[3] I assume the blockhead in question was young John. I'm glad she didn't give up.

Jesus likened soul-winning to catching fish. The fishing I have been involved with is an exercise in patience. You hang out by the water's edge, trying different types of bait and different locations. Mostly, you wait. It takes time. Conditions must be right. Sometimes you go home empty-handed. But sometimes you get a nibble.

WASH-UPS

My guess is this book will be read by faithful folks seeking to continue the spiritual legacy of Wesley. As a movement, we are aging. Many congregations realize they have long since missed their opportunity to pass their baton of faith. I have served several congregations that were a generational monolith of well-seasoned saints.

Scripture provides some encouragement. Eli, the high priest during the fading days of the period of the Judges, was a wash-up in about every way possible. His sons committed wholesale wickedness in the temple. Though he chided them for it, he didn't have the strength of resolve to stop them. He even lost the Ark of the Covenant. Losing the Ark is probably last on the list of things you should do when you are high priest. Scripture paints the portrait of Eli's waning priesthood, revealing a man frustrated, blind, and heavy in both body and fears.

But don't call Eli a failure. Through a series of miraculous events, a young boy named Samuel came into Eli's life, living with him in the temple courts. One night, the boy woke the priest. He had distinctly heard his name being called and he assumed it was the old priest needing his chamber pot. "Go back to bed. I didn't call you." Minutes later Samuel returned, reporting that he was again sure his name had been called. When it happened a third time, Eli paid attention.

Maybe, just maybe, the voice the boy was hearing was the Lord. The instructions he gave to young Samuel were simple, but effective: "If you hear the voice again, say, 'Speak, Lord, for your servant is listening.'" That night Samuel would first hear the voice of God on behalf of the nation. The timely spiritual help of a washed-up, aged priest had sparked a mighty prophet who would usher in the next era in Israel's history.

No one can ever call you a failure if you help a child discern the voice of the Lord. I challenge you to watch for the Holy Spirit's activity in a child.

To do this, we need to get to know them. We must practice patience and be willing to tell our own faith stories. In speaking of home visits, Wesley commented:

> *What patience, what love, what knowledge is required for this!*[3]

God most often speaks, as with Elijah, in "a still, small voice." The Voice can be easily missed amidst the distractions of life. As believers in prevenient grace, we trust the Holy Spirit is tugging on each heart as God draws us into relationship. Faith-sharing is not a matter of adults shoving religious ideas into young, susceptible minds. The most authentic evangelism is helping a child discern the whisper that is already there.

A spiritual mentor who helps us open our own locked doors is a powerful thing. There is something in us that wants this desperately. Scott Wilcher reminds us that our culture tells the same story over and over again through film: An orphaned child feels a nagging restlessness that the life he is living is not the one for which he was destined. A mentor suddenly appears in his life, shows him a glimpse of his true self, and ushers him into a community where his true potential can be developed.

Hagrid took Harry Potter to Hogwarts. Obi-Wan introduced Luke to the ways of the Force. Gandalf called Frodo into the Fellowship of the Ring. Morpheus helped Neo take off his blinders. Batman had Alfred. Daniel had Mr. Miyagi. Bill and Ted had Rufus. Mutants were recruited by Professor Xavier to become X-Men. Could it be that Hollywood makes billions of dollars telling these and similar stories over again because they have tapped into a deep spiritual longing within all of us?

I challenge you to watch for the child who might be struggling to make sense of the Holy Spirit's deep voice. You don't have to be a spiritual giant to help a child spiritually. You do have to know the child and be willing to speak the language of the heart when the opportunity arises. There is a space at the back of this book for you to write the name of a child you might be able to help discern the whisper in her or his heart.

[1] From *The Works of the Reverend John Wesley A.M., Volume V,* by John Emory (New York: Waugh & Mason for the Methodist Episcopal Church, 1835); pp. 216–217.

[2] From *Minutes of the Several Conversations Between The Rev. John Wesley A.M. and the Preachers in Connexion with Him, Containing the Form of Discipline Established Among the Preachers and People in the Methodist Societies* (London: 1779); p. 34.

[3] From *The Works of John Wesley, Volume 10, The Methodist Societies: The Minutes of Conference,* by Richard P. Heitzenrater (Abingdon Press: Nashville, 2011); p. 341.

"Pray in earnest for them."

–John Wesley

THREE

Pray for Them Intensely

I GREW UP on the acres of a dairy farm operated by my grandparents, Miles and Glenda Mowery. They were pillars in Cache Chapel, our tiny gravel-road United Methodist congregation deep in Southern Illinois. Grandpa was a fine example of a family man and pious in the best sense of the word. I remember him leading our family in prayer before Sunday dinner with folded hands, one of which was missing some fingers from a farm accident earlier in life. Although dairy farmers can never have a true Sabbath (the cows needing to be milked), he refrained from all unnecessary work and even from fishing on Sundays. The first day of the week was for worship and family.

Looking back, I would say that my Grandma Mowery was probably the best spiritual friend of my young life. She simply talked about the Lord, what he meant to her, and modeled a faithful life. She had a way of weaving faith stories into everyday conversation. A daughter of a "Shouting Methodist," she gave me a sense of my spiritual legacy. The holiness roots of the Second Great Awakening flowed through her to me.

But Grandma's prayers are what I remember most. Theologically speaking, it is correct to pray to God the Father in the name of Jesus. Grandma didn't do that. She talked straight to Jesus when she prayed. The way she did this left no doubt in my young heart that Jesus was leaning out over the edge of his throne to listen to her. Up into her nineties, I know she found her way to her knees at her bedside to talk to Jesus about me.

More people believe in prayer than actually practice it. A clergy mentor of mine, in a candid moment, spoke about his children: "They are good kids, but they have their struggles. I am glad their mom prays for them." Wesley, of course, listed prayer for children among our non-delegable tasks. His admonition to preachers with regards to children was to "pray in earnest for them." Among the priestly concerns of pastoral intercession is this question: "How are the kids?"

Too much of what passes for prayer for our kids is really just "worrying on our knees." When our children overhear us praying for them, do they assume the highest goal in life is not to have anything bad happen to us? There is nothing wrong with praying for divine protection, but we must not lose the Kingdom of God as the central, splendid vision of the Christian life. We should express concern for our children's character and calling, not just his or her comfort.

How should we pray? Scriptural prayers draw on God's attributes and promises as the basis of our intercession. Specific prayers dare to go beyond vague platitudes (like "bless them") to focus on particular needs. Bold prayers come from those not afraid to believe God for big things. Faith-filled prayers trust God enough to allow God to take our children through difficulty if that is a necessary step toward their sanctification, kingdom usefulness, and ultimate joy in heaven.

Because praying well for someone often leads to praying with them, we should also cultivate the gift of leading children in prayer. One way to pray with them is simply to bless them in Jesus' name. It was said of Wesley that "he always had a smile and a kind word for the children, and his manner was to place his hands on their heads and give them his heavenly benediction." There are also many examples of his praying with children who approached him following his sermons. He led them to repentance and faith through prayer. Those unable to lead another person in prayer will always have limited usefulness in the Kingdom of God.

Just as his brother Charles wrote a collection of hymns for use by children, John Wesley authored a collection of prayers for them. In the preface he wrote,

> *A lover of your soul has here drawn up a few prayers,*
> *in order to assist you in that great duty.*
> *Be sure that you do not omit, at least morning and evening,*
> *to present yourself upon your knees before God.*

If prayer is a duty, it is an agreeable one. C. S. Lewis once wrote to a friend promising his prayers for him. He added, "It is a sweet duty, praying for our friends. I always feel as if I had had a brief meeting with you when I do so: perhaps it is a meeting, and the best kind." Wesley listed prayer among the "means of grace," the channels through which God's power and mercy flow to us.

OH, SUSANNA

My Grandma Mowery was my prayer mentor. John Wesley had his mother, Susanna. It was Isaac Taylor who said the "mother of the Wesleys was the mother of Methodism."[4] She has long been recognized as a compelling example of both a saint and an educator. She was remarkable in every sense of the word.

Finding the schoolmaster in her town of Epworth to be lacking both morally and pedagogically, Susanna undertook the education of her own young children to prepare them for life and faith. John obviously considered his mother a pattern to be followed because, as an adult, he asked her to write a summary of the program of discipline and learning she employed in the home. Published under the title "The Way of Education," reveals a rigorous and deliberate pattern of spiritual formation.

Susanna had the custom of gathering her whole household together in the kitchen on Sunday nights to read a printed sermon and join in the Service of Evening Prayer from the *Book of Common Prayer*. Neighbors began to join these gatherings. When her husband, Samuel, was on an extended leave to London, he left the church in the less-than-capable hands of a paid assistant. Susanna's prayer meetings drew such a large crowd (she estimated it at two hundred or so) that the substitute priest wrote complaining to Samuel that his wife was drawing a bigger crowd in her kitchen on Sunday night than he was at church on Sunday morning. When her husband wrote to her suggesting that she dissolve her meetings, Susanna replied:

If you do, after all, think fit to dissolve this assembly,
do not tell me [merely] that you desire me to do it,
for that will not satisfy my conscience:
but send me your positive command,
in such full and express terms
as may absolve me from all guilt and punishment
for neglecting this opportunity of doing good
when you and I shall appear before the great and
awful tribunal of our Lord Jesus Christ.

The meetings continued.

It was the one-on-one mentoring by his mother that perhaps had the biggest effect on John Wesley. She dedicated one night a week to each child for a time of personal prayer, instruction, and spiritual guidance. John commented later in life how much these private lessons had meant to him. It is entirely possible that the directive for preachers to meet with children individually for spiritual training drew from his positive memories of the private time with Susanna.

The priority that Susanna gave to the spiritual life of each child was woven together with the many demands of a large family. John's father commented that his wife had given him "eighteen or nineteen children." Even he lost count! The truth is, given the high child mortality rate of the time, fewer than a dozen of the children survived to adulthood. Perhaps only six or seven lived in the home at one time. Still, her commitment to one evening a week for special instruction and individual prayer with each child was remarkable.

Susanna had a special burden for John, whom she called Jack. When a fire broke out in their parsonage, all the family escaped except for little Jackie, age five. He was spotted in a second-floor bedroom window but the stairs were by this time engulfed in flames. As neighbors ran to assist, one man stood on another's shoulders and pulled John through the window just as the roof collapsed.

Susanna, visibly pregnant at the time with her youngest child, embraced her rescued son, calling him a "brand plucked from the burning," an allusion to Zechariah 3:2.

She later wrote,

> *I determined to pray all the more diligently for him.*[5]

She believed this child had been spared for a great purpose.

A CHILD ON YOUR HEART

Our congregation recently helped start a brand new church in a neighboring city as part of our multi-site ministry. One of the first reached for Christ through this effort was a young man in his twenties. I had the honor of being present for his baptism, which was preceded by a video in which he shared his testimony of leaving his life of drugs and destructive living to come to faith in Jesus. The video was so encouraging that I showed it to my congregation the next Sunday as an example of the lives that were being changed by our new church plant.

After I shared the video in worship, a guest to our church approached me. "I am visiting from Iowa, and I want you to know that I recognize that young man. As a young boy, he attended our United Methodist Church in Iowa. His aunt is a friend of mine, and I have prayed with her for him on many occasions. I can't wait to get back home and share the news!"

As I spoke with this dear woman, I thought about the logistics the Holy Spirit had coordinated to bring about this conversation. Not only had the Spirit answered the prayers of an aunt and brought the nephew out of a life of drugs to faith in Christ, the Spirit also made sure that her friend would be visiting a church in another state on the very Sunday we were playing the video telling the story of his conversion. I can only conclude that God wanted that aunt to know that her prayers for the child God had laid on her heart had been heard and answered.

Be alert to the child God may place on your heart. Perhaps a young person comes to your mind when you pray. You might feel a special burden for a particular child or even find yourself weeping for her. This may be the Holy Spirit's call for you to pray for this child in a particular way. Write down her or his name at the back of this book and commit to pray for that child intensely.

[4] From *The Women of Methodism,* by Abel Stevens (New York: Carlton & Porter, 1866); p. 25.

[5] From *Out of Aldersgate,* by W.T. Watkins (Board of Missions, Methodist Episcopal Church, South, 1937).

*"Diligently instruct and
vehemently exhort
all parents at their own houses."*

—John Wesley

FOUR

Mentor Families Meaningfully

WE ONCE RECEIVED a complaint to our church office. A mother called to report that her child, whom she had been sending to our youth group, was using foul language at home. The parents did not attend our church but had been sending her son for several weeks and really expected better results from us. He did, after all, now profess to be a Christian. We assured her that the lad had not learned those words from us. We did remind her that we had her son for only one hour a week. Someone else had him the other one hundred sixty-seven hours. What kind of language did he hear at home?

When we minister to children, we do so humbly, realizing that the church programs do not possess anything even closely approximating the power of the home. We will do nothing but play catch-up unless we go to the source and equip parents to lead spiritually effective families. As Frederick Douglass said, "It is easier to build strong children than repair broken men." It was in this spirit that Wesley instructed Methodist preachers to

> *diligently instruct and vehemently exhort all parents.*

Not only is the home the primary unit of spiritual formation, but it is also the place where we tend to either use or lose our Christianity. Who we are at home is who we really are. Wesley realized the huge potential we have to shape the homes that shape the children. One task of home visits by Methodist preachers was to inquire into the habits and health of the family in which each child was being raised.

Taking a spiritual audit of someone else's home is not done lightly. After all, I have issues in my own home to address. But asking good questions and providing loving accountability for parents is one of the ways we bless children. During pre-baptismal instruction, I find myself growing bolder in asking direct questions about the holy habits of the family. If we don't ask the tough questions and encourage parents toward spiritual progress, who else will? In our day of traveling sports teams and competing Sunday activities for children and families, we need to have deliberate conversations with families about spiritual priorities.

MR. HENRY'S METHOD

The home where John was raised was a remarkable example of intentional spiritual formation. It was modeled from the spiritual legacy that Wesley's parents shared from their English Puritan upbringing. Although Samuel and Susanna later chose loyalty to the Established Church, they retained the best practices of their spiritual roots, including a rigorous model of spiritual parenting. A friend and contemporary of Susanna's father was a man named Philip Henry, a well-known Puritan preacher. Henry's son was the famous Bible commentator Matthew Henry, who also became his father's biographer. Wesley told his preachers to train parents in "Mr. Henry's Method of Family Prayer." This was to him the gold standard of Christian parenting and he included Henry's biography in the Christian Library he edited for his preachers and people.

Philip Henry is first described as a man who modeled private prayer and devotion. He did not try to lead his children into a faith he didn't practice himself. Not only did he maintain his own "prayer closet," but he also prayed in partnership with his wife both morning and evening:

> *It is the great duty of yoke-fellows that . . .*
> *they do all they can to help one another to heaven.*[6]

Children who see prayer at work in the lives of their parents are much more likely to pray.

Twice a day he also gathered his children and any others who might be in the household for family worship. He assembled them in the morning so that God could have the very first part of the day:

> *He that is first shall have the first.*[6]

Prayers were said, a Psalm sung, and the Scriptures were read and explained. The daily family worship was brief, not long and tedious. It was said to be a pleasure for everyone in the household.

During the evening family gathering, the prayers incorporated thoughts from the Scripture that had been read. They

> *gave thanks for family mercies, confessed family sins,*
> *and begged family blessings.[6]*

Henry prayed for each family member by name, including those who might be away. On Thursday evenings, instead of reading Scripture, he taught from the catechism. On Saturday evenings, he quizzed his children on what they had learned throughout the week. Everything was aimed at instilling in his children a love for the Holy Scriptures.

On Sundays the children were awakened with the words "The Lord is risen!" to which they would reply, "He is risen indeed!" Each Sunday was a little Easter and the house was filled with singing and Scripture. Twice the normal time was spent in family devotion in addition to attendance together at public worship. There would be a special season of prayer for the surrounding towns and villages, and the day was closed by singing Psalm 139.

If all this sounds rather monastic, it was unapologetically so:

> *He who would make his house a little church*
> *shall find that God will make it a little sanctuary.[6]*

Henry was the benevolent high priest of his home. His son remembered him as one who

*ruled and kept up his authority, but it was with wisdom and love,
and not with a high hand. He allowed his children a great degree
of freedom, which gave him the opportunity of reasoning, not
frightening them into that which is good.*[6]

Henry would regularly remind his children of their baptisms as infants
and the fact that they belonged to the Lord. To aid in this, he drew up
a short Baptismal Covenant which they were encouraged to recite from
memory each Sunday evening:

*I take God the Father to be my Chief Good, and Highest end.
I take God the Son to be my Prince and Savior.
I take the Holy Ghost to be my Sanctifier,
Teacher, Guide, and Comforter.
I take the Word of God to be my rule in all my actions.
I take the people of God to be my people in all conditions.
I likewise devote and dedicate unto the Lord my whole self,
all I am, all I have, and all I can do.
And this I do deliberately, sincerely, freely, and forever.*[6]

When the children were raised and ready to leave home, he had them
write out their covenant and sign it, so that he could remind them of their
commitment if they ever strayed.

Wesley expected that every Methodist preacher be a certified instructor in
Henry's Method for Family Prayer. He expected every Methodist home to
be an incubator for intentional discipleship.

FEELING ROTTEN

Did I mention that Philip Henry also taught his oldest daughter to read the Old Testament in Hebrew when she was seven years old? Are you feeling horrible about your own parenting yet? It is worth studying what Wesley viewed as the ideal pattern for the Christian home. We also need to talk about reality. Building holy habits into a family can be like trying to nail Jell-O to the wall, especially once other patterns are set. Most of us feel successful if we sit down and eat a meal together every once in a while with the cell phones turned off. Mr. Henry never had to contend with Snapchat.

Lois was a dear woman in a church I served. Her husband was an unbeliever and she recalled her struggles earlier in life trying to give a spiritual foundation to her three young sons. She decided one Christmas to read the story of Jesus' birth from Luke 2 before the family opened their gifts. The lads were extraordinarily active on normal days and even more so with a Christmas-induced sugar high. Shepherds keeping watch over their flocks by night was the last thing on their minds. Lois explained how she sat on the floor with one squirming boy pinned under each of her legs while she locked the third under her free arm and tried to read to them about peace on Earth. Suffice it to say the image was not something from Currier and Ives.

Wise parents, like Mr. Henry, start with themselves. Our children are more observant than we realize and our own habits speak loudly. I often tell parents that when we say something is important but act otherwise, our kids will have us figured out by age two. When the time is right, involve everyone in the family in taking a spiritual audit of the home. Identify the habits that take your family closer to God and those that take you further away. Let Scripture inform this process. Add and subtract as the Holy Spirit leads. Don't be ashamed of small beginnings or incremental steps. Consistency is more important than perfection.

Wesley's admonition to parents was persistence and resolve. In his sermon "On Obedience to Parents" he reminded dads and moms that they can do all things through Christ who strengthens them (Phil. 4:13). Be encouraged that God will intervene to transform our families if we invite God to do so. When the Holy Spirit moves, dramatic change can happen quickly.

Our hope should be that our children outrun us in our pursuit of Jesus. My sister and her husband taught tithing to their children. Because the only income they had was their allowance and birthday money, the kids were encouraged to take ten percent of this and give it to God through their church. My niece and nephews learned both the joy of giving and the ability to do with less. On their own, they decided that if ten percent was good, twenty percent was better. They started giving God a double tithe, and this has continued into their young adulthood.

EXCEPTIONAL PROMISE

The type of parenting espoused by Wesley really doesn't make much sense if all you want is to raise kids who are nice, believe in the existence of God, and don't cuss much. I dare say that this is the extent of the vision most Christian folks have for their kids. Wesley, however, envisioned our homes producing world-changing disciples. There was a day when the church strove to produce its best and brightest for the mission field. If our families are effective, we will produce young adults with exceptional skills who are ready to use their talents in radically counter-cultural ways.

If any generation of the church needed a fresh crop of spiritual giants it is this one. Which home will produce the next John Wesley, Billy Graham, or Martin Luther King Jr.? We need another Katherine Booth, Fanny Crosby, and Teresa of Calcutta. We need minds like C. S. Lewis and passionate evangelists like Phoebe Palmer and Peter Cartwright. Not only do we long for exceptional church leaders, but we also need people ardently living out their faith as teachers, physicians, business leaders, scientists, engineers, attorneys, and politicians.

Keep an eye out for the child who shows exceptional promise. Look for a sharp mind, engaging personality, and capacity to lead others. Write down her name at the back of this book. Pour a little extra into her. Plant a seed in her heart that God might have given her more because more is expected. And let's mentor families to produce world-changing disciples of Jesus Christ.

[6] All of the quotes of Phillip Henry come from Volume 28 of the 30-volume edition of *John Wesley's Christian Library*. Most are from Chapter Four of the "Life of Phillip Henry" in Volume 28.

"Some will say,
'I have no gift for this.'
Gift or no gift, you are to do this,
or else you are not called
to be a Methodist Preacher."

—John Wesley

FIVE

Challenge Ourselves Continually

OR ELSE. Here are two little words that, when placed together, command our attention. Parents employ these words upon a child unenthusiastic about cleaning his room. The government uses these words on those indisposed to pay their taxes. Even God used them from time to time.

One hearing "or else" might be tempted to call them a threat. The one delivering the words would simply describe them as a needful summary of impending consequences. The net result is a metaphorical kick in the pants. Even the best of us sometimes need this. I know that I am often hesitant to obey the voice of the Holy Spirit. How about you? We reluctant souls are in the company of the saints like Moses, who was loath to carry God's message of deliverance back to Egypt; and Jonah, who headed west for Tarshish when God called him east to Nineveh; as well as Gideon, Jeremiah, and Ananias, who each offered excuses before their ultimate obedience.

John Wesley seemed to understand that most people don't naturally line up on their own to minister to children. His "or else" to preachers is designed to help them overcome their native reluctance.

We are called to ministry with children "gift or no gift." As wonderful and needful as spiritual gifts are to the church, the lack of these gifts is not a legitimate excuse for non-participation. I think of the words of the Wesleyan Covenant Prayer that reminds us that some tasks to which we are called seem contrary to our inclinations:

> *Christ has many services to be done: some are easy,*
> *others are difficult; some bring honor, others bring reproach;*
> *some are suitable to our natural inclinations and material*
> *interests, others are contrary to both; in some we may please*
> *Christ and please ourselves; in others we cannot please Christ*
> *except by denying ourselves. Yet the power to do all these things*
> *is given to us in Christ, who strengthens us.*[7]

To minister to children as we ought, we are going to need to stretch ourselves. We need to move past our comfort, over our excuses, outside our perceived gifts, and beyond the limits of our current organization. In his work to improve healthcare systems, Dr. Paul Batalden has commented,

"Every system is perfectly designed to get the results it gets."

If you don't have many children in your life or your church, you need to realize that you are unconsciously engineered for that result. Is it time for a redesign?

GO FISH

I once had the opportunity to visit Oratorio Don Bosco de Sor Maria Romero, a Roman Catholic social service agency ministering to homeless or partially homeless children in San Jose, Costa Rica. The oratory is a day center where children can come off the street and find a safe place with food and other forms of practical assistance. I asked a staff member of the ministry how children find their way in. While some came on their own, he described how volunteers of the ministry drive through the slums looking for young people at risk: "We go fishing for children."

The phrase "fishing for children" stuck with me. Most churches say they want children. But do we fish? It seems to me we harvest only the low-hanging fruit by sticking to the children whose families bring them to church. There are kids we are not influencing that we could be if we changed business as usual, got out of our comfort zone, and extended our reach.

For eight years I served New Bethel United Methodist Church in Glen Carbon, Illinois, a growing suburban bedroom community of the St. Louis metro area with great schools, many young families, and above-average incomes. We were a comfortable, busy, growing church with lots of kids and quality children's ministries.

Twenty minutes away, however, were children living in some of the most desperate poverty to be found in the United States. Washington Park, a community in the East St. Louis School District, had a median household income less than a third of that of Glen Carbon and was rife with crime, drugs, and desperation.

With some encouragement from my wife, Becky, our congregation decided to do an extra week of vacation Bible school each summer. After our week of ministry in Glen Carbon, we would pack up all the decorations, crafts, and curricula and take them to Grace United Methodist Church in Washington Park. It was a lot of work at a time when our key people were already exhausted from the week before. The laborers were faithful, but few. However, lives were changed when we went fishing.

An observation: Poor children are not that difficult to reach. Their parents, often single mothers, are happy for good Christian folks to take an interest in their children by providing environments for them. Frankly, they need the break! Children of affluent families are heavily scheduled in sports and extracurricular activities. Poor kids have time on their hands. The church just needs to organize to receive and love children who are from a different reality. Again, we must expand the definition of "our kids."

Churches that fish do things differently. They own a used school bus to pick children up on Sundays. They put out fliers for summer programs. They serve meals at some of their ministries because some kids come hungry. They are on a first-name basis with the social workers in the schools to help identify children at risk.

I am blessed to serve a church with a lot of young families. In addition to baptizing infants, we like to make a fuss when a newborn baby is brought to our church for the first time. When new parents come forward to show off the new addition to our church family, I remind the congregation of our simple church growth strategy: "Bring one or have one."

Even better than programs reaching children outside the church is a church-wide culture of fishing for children. What if trips to church were not complete without someone in tow? How many homes with unchurched children do we pass on our way to church? How can we find out? What would it take to reach them?

THEY LAUGHED AT THEM

We should all know the name Sophia Cooke Bradburn. As a young woman, Sophia lived in the same house as the elderly John Wesley. He would greet her cheerfully each morning with a big smile and the words, "Sophy, live today!" She took his advice. It was a suggestion by Sophia that started a ministry tsunami that reached countless millions of children around the world.

Sophia became acquainted with Robert Raikes, a faithful Anglican layman, who once asked her what should be done for all the ragged children in the streets of London. Her answer: "Let's teach them to read and take them to church." That is what they did. Sophia became perhaps the world's first Sunday school teacher.

As she and Mr. Raikes marched the children to church for the first time, people on the sidewalks laughed at what seemed to them a miserable little parade of urchins. Some called the nascent movement "Raikes' Ragged Schools." Why teach these children to read who were only destined for manual labor? Some criticized the effort as a desecration of the Sabbath.

One bishop raised concern that the children could be indoctrinated into a dangerous political ideology. Fishing for children persisted in spite of heckles from the cheap seats.

That first "Sunday Charity School" was in 1780. Soon thereafter, John Wesley made it famous by publishing an article highlighting the ministry in *Arminian Magazine*. By 1821, roughly a fourth of the children in England, 1.25 million, were in a Sunday school. This paved the way for universal education of children, something we today take for granted. A simple suggestion propelled by the wind of the Holy Spirit caused church buildings that were idle on Sundays apart from worship to be filled with children in need. Wesley's journals in his later years are replete with comments about the hundreds of children he witnessed being taught in the burgeoning Sunday school movement.

In most places today, Sunday school has become ingrown and is dying. Megachurches are drawing young families and have large, polished programs for children, but how often does their reach extend to kids whose parents won't be coming to church? Maybe our generation is waiting for the next Sophy to voice a simple plan for filling our churches with children who would otherwise not hear the Gospel.

I continue to believe there are children within the reach of each congregation ... if, that is, we ready ourselves to go fishing. Unreached children today may not be playing in the streets. They are more likely parked in front of a television with a bag of Cheetos. Maybe we reach them by knocking on doors. Maybe we need to throw a block party in their neighborhood. Maybe there is a way to serve them through the schools like tutoring or after-school programs. What if we asked parents how we could help? What if we asked the kids?

Picture a child you might be tempted to consider unreachable, seemingly unlikely to ever darken the doorstep of your church. He or she can serve to fuel your imagination. Let your heart imagine Christians organized to reach this child. What kind of church are they? What do they do that your congregation would not? Write down the name of a seemingly unreachable child in the back of this book.

One thing is certain: It will be far easier to just stay comfortable and leave children unreached. If we do, John Wesley only asked that we not call ourselves Methodists.

[7] From *The Book of Public Prayers and Services for the Use of the People Called Methodist* (London: Wesleyan-Methodist Book Room, 1883); p. 284.

*"Do it as you can,
till you can do it as you would.
Pray earnestly for the gift,
and use every help
God hath put into your way,
in order to attain it."*

–John Wesley

SIX

Shape Our Ministries Appropriately

ARE YOU GOING on to perfection? Wesley expected all Methodists to be in a continuous spiritual improvement cycle. The language of our heritage is rich with phrases like "going on," "pressing forward," "hungering after," and "groaning toward." Each of us is to be progressing toward the likeness of Jesus. Movement is who we are and what we do.

Wesley insisted there was nothing innovative about his basic message. He saw himself as a purveyor of the classic Christianity handed down from the apostles. He did, however, admit that Methodists were "irregular" in terms of their methodology. They did things no one else would do in order to reach people no one else was reaching. Part of being a people on a journey is freely adapting our delivery of the classic message for an ever-changing landscape.

Wesley told his preachers to constantly improve their ministry with children. His prescription was not to study how to develop some ideal model. Pressing toward perfection is not the same thing as perfectionism. No, he told us to jump in and improve as we go.

> *Do as you can, until you can do it as you would.*

We'll get better as we go along. Prayer and perspiration go together like breathing in and breathing out. Wesley hinted that God would put some help in our path along the way. You can only steer a ship that is moving.

Constant improvement is required because ministry to children always presents fresh challenges. Kids themselves are in a constant state of change called growing up. Today they develop within the context of a culture that is evolving faster than any in history. A church that reaches beyond its membership will also interact with family systems that are very different from our own. Ministry to children will always be a cross-cultural experience because kids are plugged into media and technology we don't always understand.

The most authentic children's ministry is a lifestyle, not a program. But the programs we offer are vitally important. The late Bishop Rueben Job left a great gift to the church in his book *Three Simple Rules*. This study in the General Rules of the Methodist Societies gives us a grid from which to evaluate our ministry to kids:

Do no harm. Do good. Stay in love with God.

We'll begin with the last one.

HELP CHILDREN STAY IN LOVE WITH GOD

When we baptize a baby, the parents make promises to reject evil, accept God's help, live under the lordship of Jesus, and stay in the fellowship of the church. The church also has promises to make. We agree to pray for the family, receive the child into our care, and be an example to the child as he or she grows. I sometimes take the occasion of an infant baptism to remind the church of the joyful burden we are accepting. These children we mark are going to need adults who care enough to get trained in our child protection policies. They are going to need caring nursery volunteers to change their diapers and faithful Sunday school teachers who come to church early and stay late. They will need people to save oatmeal containers for their vacation Bible school crafts. Someone is going to have to bake the cookies, as well. They will need youth leaders and someone to change the oil on the church van before mission trips. The whole congregation is needed if we are going to do this well and continually do it better.

Every once in a while we need to take a collective pause and evaluate how we are doing. Bishop Job gives us the right question: Are children falling in love and staying in love with God? Wesley wanted every child to know the foundational truths of the Gospel. They should memorize the Apostles' Creed, understand God's holy commandments, and know what Jesus has accomplished to reconcile us to God. They need to learn to serve others and serve with others as a path toward Christian humility. We should be seeing hearts of children grow larger and larger with love for God and neighbor.

Do not dismiss the importance of counting the number of children involved in our ministries. Do numbers matter? It depends on what we are counting. When counting children, I would say numbers matter greatly. If fewer children are being engaged with what we are doing, we need to make adjustments in our approach. Wesley never stuck with a ministry model that was not working for the sake of tradition and neither should we.

I have served some very quiet and orderly churches in my ministry. When we shuffled in on Sunday morning things were just as we had left them the week before. During silent prayer you could hear our bones creek. I will take a noisy church any day of the week. Give me juice box stains on the carpet. I'll take goldfish cracker crumbs in the pews. I am more than happy to preach over squalling babies. I like it when there are so many kids running around the fellowship space that it looks like a freshly-kicked ant hill. I don't agree that kids are the church of tomorrow. They are the church of today. But a church without them doesn't have a tomorrow.

DO NO HARM TO CHILDREN

In the last chapter, I talked about "fishing for children" by reaching beyond our comfort zone in order to minister to them. As we do so, we must also remember that we are not the only ones with our lines in the water. Children are at daily risk from predatory forces. I think of bullying, verbal and physical abuse, forms of exploitation, and marketing to children things destructive to them.

> *Jesus saved his direst warnings for those who might do children harm: "If any of you put a stumbling block before one of these little ones who believe in me, it would be better for you if a great millstone were fastened around your neck and you were drowned in the depth of the sea" (Matthew 18:6).*

Certainly followers of Jesus should be more proactive in protecting and seeking the good of children than those who would seek to do them harm.

Because the church is made up of human beings, everything "out there" in our culture is also inside the church. We all are sinners and have the potential for great harm. This is why we must watch over one another in love. My wife, Becky, instituted the first "Safe Sanctuary" policy in the church I serve as a way of limiting the potential for harm within our ministries to children and youth. We are aware that those prone to prey upon children sometimes use church environments to groom their next victims.

A hard-working, Gospel-centered church will not allow the potential for abuse to become an excuse for inactivity. They choose instead to operate wisely, create safety in numbers, and establish healthy boundaries. When meeting with a child privately for spiritual conversation, they do so within view of other adults who know they have a role in protecting children from harm and adults from accusation. Two adults unrelated to each other stay with the children at all times or else there is a "roamer" going from room to room to keep an eye on things. Classroom doors must have windows. Car rides are only within certain parameters. Most of this is just good, old-fashioned common sense.

In the church I serve we refuse to ignore suspicions of abuse. We have found the local police to be very capable partners in protecting both our children and our ministry. We trust them to filter through the information we provide. We also partner with school social workers and other folks with a shared interest in promoting the well-being of children. Protecting kids is a team effort.

Because kids can also hurt one another, it is urgent that we not only teach the Golden Rule but make sure it is modeled in our ministry environments. We confront bullying and encourage sensitivity in children to the feelings of others. We raise our children to be protectors as well as protected. The teachings of Jesus are, after all, relevant on the elementary school playground, in social media, and at the middle school lunchroom table.

DO GOOD TO CHILDREN

Thomas Rutherford, an early Methodist preacher, traveled with John Wesley and later shared stories from his life. He once told about riding with Wesley near Glasgow, Scotland, when they noticed a girl without shoes or socks. Wesley dismounted, called the child over, gave her some money (he often saved his shiniest coins to give to children he would meet), and spoke some words of encouragement to her.

As the preachers continued their journey, Wesley told his companion a story from his time as a young missionary priest in America. Wesley was teaching at a school in Savannah and his good friend, Charles Delamotte, taught at another. One day Delamotte explained to Wesley that some of the boys in his school could afford shoes and socks and some could not. Those with shoes cruelly ridiculed those without. He sharply put a stop to this whenever he heard it, but discerned that the mistreatment continued when he was not around. He was at a loss to know what to do.

Wesley told his friend that he thought he could correct the situation if they traded teaching posts for one week. On the appointed day, Wesley showed up at Delamotte's school to teach the boys... barefooted. He recalled how the students looked at him and then at each other with surprise. He went right to the lessons for the day without comment. Throughout the week of John Wesley's barefoot lectures, he noticed that the boys without shoes carried their heads a little higher. By the end of the week, those with shoes were leaving them at home to be more like their instructor.

Children need an advocate, an adult who is seeking their good. Sometimes this involves defending them, sometimes providing for them, and sometimes simply expecting the best from them.

Throughout my growing-up years, I had an Aunt Lida. She wasn't really my aunt. She was a friend and mentor of my mother from her days as a young school teacher. She and my mom continued their friendship and, around the time of my birth, Lida decided to be my Aunt Lida. A few days before my birthday each year, a card or package would arrive in the mail addressed to "Master Christopher Miles Ritter." Yes, Master. I never figured out what I was the master of, but it was empowering to see my name written in that way. I always somehow knew to use my best manners with Aunt Lida although she never reminded me to do so. She simply expected more from me.

By the standards of my family, Aunt Lida was wealthy. She didn't, however, shower me with expensive presents. She gave me thoughtful gifts that had something to do with my development. She bought me things like stationary. When you are an eight-year-old boy, you don't get really excited about stationary. But my first "thank you" notes were written on the clown-patterned paper and envelopes she provided. She knew letter writing would be a life skill that would serve me well throughout my days.

An advocate is one who simply seeks the good of another. I have a friend who does this through the Big Brothers Big Sisters organization. He invites his adopted little brother into his own family activities and gives him opportunities that he otherwise would not have. Wesley was a proponent of quality godmothering and godfathering. It is always a win for a child when an adult makes the commitment to invest in his or her journey.

Keep an eye out for a child needing an advocate, whether as a protector, as a provider, or as someone committed to an ongoing investment in his or her development. Write the child's name in the space provided at the back of this book. Do them good. Prevent their harm. Help them to stay in love with God.

*"Preach expressly
on the education of children
when you make the Collection
for Kingswood School."*

—John Wesley

SEVEN

Care for Them Practically

YOU DON'T KNOW the story of Methodism until you know the story of a place called Kingswood. This regal-sounding name is a hold-over from Norman and Saxon times when the forested area was used as a royal hunting estate. By Wesley's day, however, it was perhaps the most un-royal place in all of England. About three miles from the large city of Bristol, the landscape of Kingswood was cratered with seventy pits. Migrant squatters living in the forest subsisted by digging out coal from the pits and hauling it to the city for fuel.

The soot-covered Kingswood coal miners (a.k.a. colliers) were considered by many as little better than beasts. They had their own heavy dialect that was difficult for outsiders to understand. They had no church or school. The authorities considered the area ungovernable. An effort to install a toll booth along the road between Kingswood and Bristol to raise revenue for the maintenance of the road resulted in its demolition by mob action. There were times when residents of Kingswood rioted in Bristol and soldiers from London had to be dispatched to restore order.

John Wesley's friend and colleague George Whitefield was in the Bristol area in 1739 speaking in churches about his imminent American mission to convert the heathen. Some of his friends challenged him that if heathens were what he was looking for, he need look no further than the colliers of Kingswood. These were worse than any of the "savages" he might encounter in America. Why not go preach to them?

Whitefield took the dare. A month earlier he had preached outside a church building for the first time when such a large crowd came to hear the fiery young orator that they were unable to fit inside the sanctuary. He moved his sermon out to the churchyard cemetery. This highly irregular practice raised eyebrows and he was sharply criticized for it. In Kingswood, he would go yet a step further by daring to preach on unhallowed ground.

Whitefield arrived unannounced and preached the gospel to two hundred curious residents on February 17, 1739. The impromptu sermon was the first instance of "field preaching" in the Methodist revival, a strategy that would become a hallmark of the movement. This "vile" practice would eventually get Whitefield, the Wesleys, and their band of young preachers banned from many respectable churches.

The residents of Kingswood, however, were quite receptive to Whitefield's gospel news, the message that we have no righteousness of our own but, through Jesus' love and sacrifice, are given a fresh start with God as a free gift. After his first impromptu sermon, Whitefield announced he would be back on an appointed day. This next time thousands came to listen. The Holy Spirit showed up, too. The tears painting white streaks down the dirty faces of the Kingswood colliers were the first drops in the spiritual monsoon that would come to be known in America as the Great Awakening and in England as the Evangelical or Methodist Revival.

Whitefield soon took the novelty of field preaching to a bowling green in Bristol, England's second city. Although he lost some friends in doing so, God did a similar work with the people there. Whitefield's journals record crowds of around twenty thousand people coming to hear him. While there was no particular "altar call" given, people cried out to God for mercy, fell to the ground, or shook violently under the conviction of the Holy Spirit. Over the next six weeks of ministry, it was apparent that something new and powerful was breaking loose.

The problem was that Whitefield had immediate plans to embark for America. He wrote to his friend John Wesley, who had only recently had his own heart-warming Aldersgate experience, to come help. Wesley was a stranger in Bristol, but Whitefield introduced him as a worthy leader to continue the work that he had begun. It was on Monday, April 2, at a brickyard in Bristol that Wesley first "consented to be more vile" and followed Whitefield's practice of preaching outdoors. Tens of thousands of such sermons were to follow over his long ministry. Wesley would better capitalize on the impact of the outdoor gatherings by organizing those affected into a society so that a more lasting work of the Holy Spirit could take root. It was in the Bristol society that the first Methodist class meetings evolved.

The week following his first open-air sermon, Wesley preached in Kingswood to great effect. By November of that year, he could report the transformation of the entire area:

Kingswood does not now, as a year ago, resound with cursing and blasphemy. It is no more filled with drunkenness and uncleanness, and the idle diversions that naturally lead thereto. It is no longer full of wars and fightings, of clamour and bitterness, of wrath and envyings. Peace and love are there. Great numbers of the people are mild, gentle, and easy to be entreated. They "do not cry, neither strive," and hardly is their "voice heard in the streets," or indeed in their own wood, unless when they are at their usual evening diversion—singing praise unto God their Savior.[8]

Another notable first in Kingswood was the "watch night." These meetings are today associated with New Year's Eve services of covenant renewal. They started, however, among the coal miners in 1740 as an alternative gathering for those who no longer wanted to lie drunk in gin houses on Saturday nights. They gathered instead to pray and sing through the night. Kingswood has been called "the rough cradle in which Methodism was first nursed and rocked."

What does all this have to do with ministering to children? Kingswood was the location of Methodism's very first social service institution. It is sometimes said that the Methodists built a school before they ever built a church, and this is practically true. As the first Methodist meetinghouse was being built in Bristol in 1739, Wesley was overseeing the construction of a school in Kingswood for the children of the colliers. Wesley gave it a commission from Luke 19:

that their children, too, "might know the things which make for their peace."

The two-room school would be a place where volunteer teachers would instruct children of the colliers in the morning and adults in the afternoons after work. In 1748, a larger boarding school was built nearby, mainly for the children of Methodist preachers. It was this "new school" in Kingswood that Wesley once said he had spent more of his time on than any other project and for which he encouraged funds to be raised annually.

THE WHOLE GOSPEL

Understanding the story of Kingswood helps us map the genome of our spiritual DNA. For Wesleyans, there is no division made between the salvation of souls, physical well-being, and intellectual health. Everything is connected. Caring for someone's physical needs without attending to their spirit is as misguided as preaching to them without showing care for their physical well-being. John Wesley expected us to care for children practically as well as spiritually.

I serve a church that decided that no child in our community should be without a decent bed. We designated our Easter mission offering to this cause and formed a partnership with the local food pantry. Whenever there is a need, a team from our church delivers a new covered mattress, box springs, bed frame, pillows, and a warm blanket sewn by members of our congregation. With permission from the family, the team prays for the home before they leave.

I was driving through a fast food restaurant recently and a woman grabbed for my hand through the serving window. She was a single mom working for minimum wage, and her sons had been the recipients of new beds from our church. She explained how their old stained mattresses had holes stuffed with rags in an attempt to make them level. Another mother commented that her child had been sleeping on the floor.

Sheryle, a member of our church, birthed a ministry to kids called "Backpack Blessings." Volunteers pack bags of food each week for children deemed by our local school district as needing help. This extra food slipped privately into their backpacks is designed to help them through the weekend when school lunches are not available. Backpack Blessings is now supported by several churches in our community and has expanded to other area school districts.

Perhaps the most holistic way to love a child is through adoption. It was gratifying to be the pastor of New Bethel UM Church as the members of the congregation had a culture of adoption. In addition to domestic adoptions, almost every continent of the world was represented in our congregation through international adoptions.

The church I presently serve has a heart for supporting children in the state foster-care system. There are over 100,000 kids in foster care in the U.S. eligible for adoption. There are around 250,000 Christian churches in the U.S. What if more churches better organized to support foster and adoptive parents? I noticed in my trips to Africa that nearly every Christian family there had children living with them who were not biologically part of their nuclear family.

West Point is a slum on the outskirts of Monrovia, Liberia, situated on a small peninsula jutting out into the Atlantic Ocean. Tightly-packed tin hovels, the vast majority without sanitation, are home to perhaps 75,000 people. A United Nations report counts no more than four public toilets serving the entire population. Everyone uses the beach as their toilet. People also fish for herring on this same beach.

West Point is the worst slum in the poorest nation in the poorest region of the world. It is known for crime, drugs, disease, prostitution, and desperation. In 2014 it was ground zero for the Ebola outbreak.

I visited West Point in 2012 and found God's people there. We drove through narrow crowded streets and arrived at John Kofi Asmah United Methodist Church. The congregation stacked their pews at the back of their humble sanctuary each week and used chalkboards as room dividers so children in the community could have classrooms in which to learn.

Associate Pastor Sam Quarshie introduced us to some orphans who were wards of the congregation and then asked us to follow him further into West Point on foot. A tight labyrinthine path led us through a patchwork of small, open-air tin homes and past clumps of smoldering rusty barrels over which herring was being smoked. We startled more than one of the residents there with the sudden appearance of our white faces. Turning a corner we ourselves were startled to see a new three-story concrete building rising before our eyes. This was the new home of John Kofi Asmah United Methodist School, a project done in partnership with the Illinois Great Rivers Conference of the UMC and built on donated land.

Future students of the new school had hauled in buckets of sand by hand to mix the concrete needed for the project. When it was complete, it was the only school in West Point that extended through the junior high level. They hope to soon expand their schedule so that they can begin serving as a high school in the afternoon.

I think John Wesley would recognize John Kofi Asmah United Methodist School as a worthy successor to the school he built in Kingswood in 1739.

If Methodism was born by someone taking the gospel and practical assistance somewhere no one else wanted to go, maybe it could be reborn that same way. My two brief trips to Africa have impressed upon me that there are whole nations of impoverished children. So many children! It is no wonder that the developing world is referred to by some missiologists as the "Three-Fourths world." Seventy-five percent of human beings live in the Global South. The vast majority of babies are born there. The Western church needs to be invested in these places where the greatest need collides with the largest population of children. Their future is the future of Christianity and the entire planet.

Working in Africa has taught me that everything is usually about twice as difficult as you think it is going to be. The needs are so great and the cultural differences so profound that simply throwing a little money around at a few worthy projects really doesn't accomplish much. It takes relationships, commitment, and the right partners. Sustainability is a huge issue. After more than a decade of involvement, I can honestly say that the investment in worthwhile.

Picture the eyes of a child in Africa, South America, or Asia. What could you do to impact their need for clean water, food, education, clothing, or health care? There is no need to reinvent the wheel. The mission agency of your church or denomination might already be positioned to help you. Give the child you picture in your mind a name and write it in the back of this book. Alternatively, you might know a child much closer to home who needs your help. Let the list of seven names you wrote become a daily part of your prayer life. Give God your availability, and watch how the Holy Spirit will use you to reach them.

People have been predicting the demise of Methodism since it began. Near the end of his life, John Wesley was asked by a younger preacher: "What advice can you give in order to continue the great revival of which you have been the principal instrument?" His brief answer was the same instruction he had given to his preachers years earlier. I trust he would say the same thing to us today:

> *"Take care of the rising generation."*
>
> —*John Wesley*

---

[8] From *The Journal of The Rev. John Wesley A.M. Volume I* (London: J. Kershaw, 1827); p. 241.

CHILDREN GOD IS CALLING YOU TO REACH:

A child I know who is on his or her tiptoes, ready to be taught:

_____

A child I may be able to help discern the voice of the Holy Spirit:

_____

A child God has placed on my heart for particular prayer:

_____

A child whose exceptional potential I can encourage:

_____

A child difficult to reach:

_____

A child who needs an advocate:

_____

A child whose basic needs are not met:

_____

"All your children shall be taught by the LORD, and great shall be the peace of your children." Isaiah 54:13 (ESV)